STOCK INVESTING

How To Invest In Stocks: A Complete And Practical Guide For Beginners And Intermediates

Adrian McNulty

Table of Contents

INTRODUCTION

How do I start investing with little money?

You might be wondering if it possible to start investing with little money. Well, this is absolutely possible. You do not need thousands or millions of dollars to start investing. All you will require is a good plan, with which you can start investing at low as with only $50 every month.

In order to accumulate wealth successfully, you should be very keen and disciplined when it comes to developing investing habits. A wise person will start immediately regardless of their financial ability and aim to improve day by day. Sooner than ever, you will be very strong and financially stable to expand your investments the way you want. Though with a little money start, you will be able to diversify your investment risks, broaden your investment horizons and more so, develop an investing habit.

What it means by little money investment

Well, little money could be defined as something definitely not more than $1000. This could be as little as $5 depending on the kind of start that you want. With such a parameter in mind, you can let your money grow as fast as you could ever imagine by investing in different lines that you prefer. As a little money investor, you are required to be very keen in avoiding principal losses as this may get you to a zero level

Investing with little money

Today, there are various trading apps that will need you to start investing with as little as only $5. However, be sure that this will help you to reap very little hence you need to add your capital as you progress. Such trading apps with as low as $5 investments show a listing for various little money funding. With low fund wishing to grow your investment faster, you could consider owning stock with a group of investors. This will help to diversify your funds as well as reduce risk chances

With $100-$500 you can choose exchange traded funds; ETFs or the divided reinvesting plans, (DRIPs). If you are decided to invest in a particular company, you can invest your stocks. The DRIPs and ETFs are preferred by most beginners and those with little money as they allow diversification and reduces chances of making losses.

More so, you need to note that making direct investment to a particular company may be detrimental. This is like putting your all eggs in a single basket as they may all break at once. In case your ideal company gets a financial trouble and you have all your investments there, then you get into a devastating loss.

Saving to invest

When you're starting at a low investment cost, it is important to consider saving more and more. In fact, saving is an investing method since, you need to save to invest. All you need to make a simple start and learn to make it a habit.

You can save on daily, weekly or monthly basis depending on your plan. In case you start with a dollar a day, this could add up to $360 within a single year and more basing on what you save. To easily have something to save, you need to learn to spend less than what you earn.

How to invest with little money

Being fully informed will give you the ability to invest successfully. With the advanced technology, there are so many brokerage firms that offer discount. All you need is to understand the market trend and go for the one that suits your personal preferences. Note that brokerage apps are being invented day after another. Be keen and take time to research on various investment apps available today to ensure that you are able to fare well. 3

Little money investment options

As an investor with little money, you are will have overwhelming options to choose from before you decide on which to go for. Most of the little money investors have no brokers hence they are required to do all the basic research by themselves. Below are some little money investments that may make you a tomorrows millionaire if done with diligence.

1. Automatic Investments

The Hedgeable, Betterment, Wealthfront, and the WiseBanyan are among the top best Robo advisors that can help you to deal with automatic investments successfully. Most of these investments advisors are available in investment app store in your phone or you could just search them online. You can find many of these advisors online or in your phone's app store. What the online advisors do is that they manage your account portfolio requiring you to only take the responsibility of account funding. What happens here is that, you assign on your monthly deposit limits as an agreement with the robo advisors of your choice and they will do the management at only a small and affordable fee. It is advisable to go through the firm's agreements and requirements keenly before you commit by signing as any disagreement may lead to loss of your funds

2. Employer IRA

Never give away free money! That is exactly what an Employer-Sponsored IRA provides you. If your employer provides matching contributions, this investment is a must. Even if you only invest a small percentage of each paycheck into your IRA, it builds up over time. Generally, you should maximize your contributions to take advantage of your employer's matching contributions. If you cannot afford the maximum contribution right away, try to work up to that point.

3. Treasury Securities

Treasury securities is a possible little money investment with lower chances of risks, hence the best for many beginning investors. These securities are easily predictable since there market is constant as they do not experience any changes. According to the United States department of Treasury debt and its security holders, every security has a specific date of maturity, which ranges between a period of 30 days to as long as 30 years. Ensure to invest money which you can comfortably part with up to the date of maturity, since you cannot access it till then. On the other hand, a bill cashed earlier than the expected date may cause you a loss of losing a percentage of the principal amount.

Stock investing with little money

As discussed earlier on, there are many available brokerage firms where you can purchase individual stocks at a discount. Many discount brokerage firms make it easy to purchase individual stocks. The fees these firms charge is minimal, and it gives you a chance to own a portion of a company. If you have your heart set on a specific company, this could be an affordable way to achieve your dream.

If you want to own a portion of a stock because you have little to invest, consider DRIPs. The Dividend Reinvestment Plan allows you to start with a minimal investment and work your way up. Your reinvested dividends or contributions build up your ownership of the company's stock.

CHAPTER 1: WHY SHOULD YOU INVEST IN STOCKS?

Stocks are just one of the ways that you can use to invest your money in. It is true that investors prefer to invest in stock rather than in bonds, antique sports car, rare coins and treasury among others. This is because stocks have a higher chance of providing high potential returns. When it comes to long term investments, stocks perform exceptionally well.

As we look at why you should invest in stocks, it is also essential that we look at the disadvantages of investing in stocks. The downside of stocks is that they are unstable investments: this is due to the fact that the value of stock can decrease in the short term investment period. There are times that the prices of stock fall for a prolonged period of time; therefore you will find investors being advised to take long term investment when it comes to stocks.

Reasons to Consider Stock Investment

1. They offer more potential growth

When you compare the US stocks and the investment bonds for over a long period of time, the US stocks has constantly earned more. When we take a look at the worth of $100 in the stock market, the S&P started to track its performance since 1926. Stocks had an average of 10.01% yearly, short-term investments had 3.32% and bonds had 5.17% this was before inflation; therefore, showing that stocks have a higher potential of growth when its long term investment. Hence, investing in ETFs, mutual funds or stocks is vital especially when saving for a far-off goal or retirement.

2. You do not need to invest all your money in stocks

A proper mix of investments ought to be established depending on an individual financial situation, tolerance of risk and time horizon. Individuals with a longer investment horizon have the ability to take risks that are associated with a broad significant diverse exposure to stocks. As there is time to recover from the short term losses.

Benefits of Investing In Stocks

- Stock ownership utilizes the advantages of the growing economy. This is seen when the economy is growing, the corporate earnings grows as well. This is due to the fact that the economy grows generating income, leading to fatter paychecks which will in turn boost consumer demand. Eventually there will be more revenues driven to a company's cash registers.

- Stock market makes it easy for you to purchase shares of particular companies. You can be able to buy the shares through a broker, online or a financial planner. The moment you have an account, you will be able to purchase stocks within minutes, it is important for you to understand how investment of stocks works before you get into it.

- The stocks are easy to sell off in the stock market. This is important in cases where you might need your money urgently since the prices are unstable you may have a risk of taking a loss.

- Investing your money in stocks is one of the best ways of being ahead of inflation. The average annual return of stocks is 10%, which is much better when compared to the 3.2% annual inflation rate. Having the 10% annual returns means that you need to have a time horizon that is longer, this allows you to buy and hold stocks even when their value drops temporarily.

- You are able to make money in two ways: that is from the buy-and-hold investors and the day traders. As investors you buy stock with the hope of selling it high, thus you will find investors investing in fast-growing corporations which increase in value. There are investors who prefer to have a steady stream of cash; therefore, they get stocks from companies which pay dividends.

How They Are Easier Method of Becoming a Business Owner

When it comes to owning a business, you can do so by:

- Buying an existing business
- Buying franchise
- Taking over a family business
- Starting a new business

With the mentioned ways you can be a business owner. But you can also be a business owner by purchasing of stocks from a corporation. This is one of the simplest ways of becoming a business owner.

Being a shareholder of a company allows you be an owner of the business. A shareholder is an individual who holds shares of a company, owning of a share in a company has proprietary interest. The shares owned by a shareholder represent a portion of the company. You can be a shareholder for a company that has share capital; the following is a list of shareholders that you can become:

1. Ordinary shareholders

Shareholders here have shares with no special rights; they also have no restrictions that come with owning a share. A company main financial risk is usually sustained by these shareholders. It's also important to note that when a company is successful, they will have the greatest reward but they will also incur the greatest loss in the vent that the company is unsuccessful.

2. Preference shareholders

The shareholders here have a specific amount of participation; this can be through redemption or by dividend. The dividend paid to them has a fixed rate.

3. Founders or Deferred shareholders

The shareholders have special rights as they sold their business to the company in order to have some share in the company. When it comes to priority founders shareholders come after the ordinary shareholders.

Benefits of being a shareholder

- You will be able to get a part of the profits made by the business. This is especially so when a business makes huge profits or when the company is stable.
- You are entailed to be given notice of meetings that the company has.
- You have the right of attending company meetings and being able to vote
- You will be able to transfer your shares to another individual as they are a personal property, which can be transferred.
- You also have the right of receiving dividends when it is declared by the company.

Think Of Stocks as Cash Machines

As a winning investor you know that stocks are money machines and not slot machines. In the stock market, you can make money by buying stocks before the stock market goes up and ensure that you sell the stocks before the stock market goes down. For you to do well it is essential that you be able to predict if the stock market is going up or down.

Over the years investors have had different ways of determining the pattern of the market. As a result they came up with the following patterns:

- Markets which do well in years that end in 5; for instance 2005 and 2015
- Markets doing well in years that end with 8; for instance 2008 ad 2018
- Markets do well in dragon years which are in the Chinese calendar among others.

The main problem with the seductive pattern is that they exist in the past although they disappear when someone tries to use them. You do not need to use the mentioned patterns as there is a better way of determining the nature of the market. This is so as the market is compared to a casino, as it has the short-run outcomes which are unpredictable and the long-run outcomes which are a near certainty.

As we said earlier the stock market is similar to the casino, as investors are seduced by the worthless patterns that are present. You will also find the over cautious individuals staying away, as they fear losing their money if the stock price fall. A stock market acts as a casino, anonymous gamblers welcomes with open arms the compulsive stock traders.

In stock market, the investors have the hedge and not the house as in the case of a casino. In the market when the companies make profits they take a portion of the profits giving it to their investors as dividends. When it comes to stocks, investors tend to lose in short-run but are more likely to win in the long-run.

The secret in stock market is keeping your eyes on the long-run winning. Do not be distracted by dreams or wishes and most especially by price fluctuations of short-term periods. Have your mind on the next thirty years to come as it is worth trying it.

Stock Beat Robbing Effect of Inflation

Inflation is the rise in the prices of services and goods; inflation reduces the purchasing power that each unit of currency is able to buy a service or good. With the rise in inflation, it causes a deceptive effect that is: input prices become high consumers are able to only buy fewer goods, profits and revenues decrease and the economy will slow for some time to the point where a steady state of the market is attained.

When it comes to stock they are able to beat inflation with time. This is because, corporative can raise prices of stocks thus being able to account for the increase in cost, which is brought by inflation. When it comes to inflation, stocks are considered as the best hedge there is. This is because; stocks do not have a claim on any real assets which includes; land, equipment and plants which increase in value when there is also an increase in prices.

Diversify internationally in order to insulate your portfolio from inflation. When the inflation is kicked in to the overdrive, the dollar tends to fall and the foreign stock then acts like an automatic hedge. The money which was invested in foreign money will be translated to dollars. If you run to speculative assets, they deflate in price as the inflation slows down.

For the long term investors, their stocks will best act as an excellent hedge when the prices are rising. Stocks are bad short-term hedges in cases where the inflation is rapidly increasing; but when you compare it with bonds, bonds are the worst. When there is a rise in inflation, stock prices tend to falter because of the investors who fear that the Fed will increase interest rates.

In the event that the annual range of inflation is between 2 to 5% then stocks will still be doing well. If the inflation range is above 5% then the performance of stocks begin to falter. This will result to the stocks losing their hedging ability as the inflation sparks a high rate of interest. When calculating the prices of stock, interest rates are a key variable.

The possibility of higher interest rates tends to become bearish to the stock market. This is due to the fact that it encourages the investors to secure their cash from the equities to the less risky and more attractive securities such as the money market funds. When the funds flow into the market is low then the lower the demand for the stocks will be; thus leading to a low share price.

If the inflation continues to rise, the minimum amount of returns from stock investment will be high; thus leading to the market valuation being lower. The share prices will then decrease until the yield earnings estimated increases to the point of being able to offset the expected inflation. Making your investments in stocks a good way of hedging against inflation over long period of time.

When it comes to beating inflation, stocks are among the few assets that can rely on. You can also consider real estate which is able to track inflation through the use of value appreciation. Although, using real estates is not as liquid as when you are using stocks. This is mainly because of the fact that you may not be able to sell at your desired price when you are in need of money.

Stocks are able to beat inflation with time, mainly because corporative have the ability to increase prices so as to account for the rise in costs due to inflation. For instance, when the cost of sales and the wages rise because of inflation, companies can pass to consumers the high cost by increasing of prices with time. When the prices are increased the company's earnings and revenue also increase. This will lead to higher earnings, with a high valuation it will lead to a higher share prices.

CHAPTER 2: BASIC INFORMATION ABOUT STOCK MARKET

Stock market, which is also known as share or equity market is the accumulation of both the buyers and sellers of shares. A stock or share shows ownership of a business, it includes securities which can either be traded privately or itemized on a public stock exchange. Equity crowdfunding platform allows private companies to sell their shares to investors.

In the event that a company wants to raise some money, the company sells off some of its share to the willing investors. This is made possible by using the Initial Public Offering (IPO). The price of the shares is work out using the total worth of the company and the number of shares that is being issued out. The company keeps the money raised so as to be able to grow the enterprise.

The shares will continue trading on an exchange market for instance the New York Stock Exchange or the Nasdaq. Investors and the traders will continue to buy and sell the shares of the company on the exchange market, but the company will not be receiving money from trading of the stock. The company will only be receiving money from the IPO. The stock market does not work the same way a grocery store works, in that you cannot buy shares off the shelf.

You will to need a licensed broker for you to be able to trade on the major indexes in the market, for instance the S&P 500, New York Stock Exchange (NYSE) and the Nasdaq. The broker will in turn deal with the stock exchange on your behalf. A list of shares will be on the specific exchange market which brings the sellers and buyers together.

Individual in this market are represented by a broker who are presently online brokers. Through the broker place a stock trade, the broker will then deal with the exchanges on your behalf. Nasdaq and the NYSE open from 9.30 in the morning to 4.00 in the evening.

Depending on your broker there can be after- hours trading session and the premarket sessions available.

The Stock market indexes

When it comes to the stock market index, it tracks the performance of a particular group of stocks that is able to show a specific sector or the whole market for instance the retail companies. Therefore, when you hear that the stock market is up and down, it refers to the performance of the major market indexes. When it comes to the overall performance of the stock market, the Nasdaq composite, the Standard & Poor's 500 and the Dow Jones are used as proxy.

As an investor, you can use indexes so as to benchmark the performance of your portfolios. Through the exchange-traded funds and the index funds, you are able to invest in an entire index.

Bull markets versus bear markets

The stock market uses the bear animal as a symbol of fear. A bear markets indicates that the stock prices are falling. The onset varies although it has a tune of 20% or even more; this is across several of the indexes. Young investors are usually familiar with the term bear market although they are not familiar with the experience the market offers.

Bull market on the other hand means investors are quite confident, this indicates an economic growth. Bull markets tend to be followed by bear markets, bear markets are also followed by bull markets. The two market signals a larger economic pattern. In bear market, investors are pulling back; the best part of the two markets is that the bull market averagely outlasts the bear market.

Definition of Share of Stock

Share of stock is also known as stocks or shares; it signifies the impartiality of ownership of a particular corporation that is divided into units. Hence, multiple people are able to have a certain percentage of the business. In the event that a business wishes to merge, a corporate charter is to be filled by the state government.

Many of the corporations join and house in Delaware, this is because of the freedom that the corporation will enjoy. Not to forget the petty fees, this is a requirement by the Delaware government. In spite of this you will find a majority of the corporations are set up in their own home states.

The charter is to set the number of shares which are authorized. The number of shares that are authorized can show the number of shares available to the company. The available share is used as equity financing by the company.

Companies can issue more shares than they want, enabling them to be able to raise capital for the future from the new investors. Par value is also set for each share by the corporate charter. A par value is not a requirement that by law that companies need to set, although companies set them for various reasons.

Investors become shareholders when shares are issued to the investors by the new corporations. The issued shares are logged in a common stock equity account which is on the balance sheet. When it comes to the balance sheet, it shows the number of outstanding shares and the total number of authorized shares.

Companies have different classes of stock; the two main classes are the preferred shares and the capital stock which is also known as common shares. The common shareholders have a voting right that is equal to the percentage of their ownership; they also have an equity stake in the business. They can elect board of directors who will select executives who are to run the corporation. When it comes to preferred shareholders they do not have a voting right, although they uphold their preferred rights to the dividends that are released.

Stock Symbol

Stock symbol is also known as a ticker symbol, it is a string which consist of letters or numbers that identifies a bond, mutual fund, ETF, stock or any other security that is traded in a stock exchange market. Each and every traded stock has its own ticker symbol. When it comes to allocation of the ticker symbol, it varies from one country to the next. Some countries give 4 characters to a stock while others specify on a set of numbers as a way of identifying the stocks.

In the event that a company is issuing out securities to the public, it will need to select an exchange where the securities will trade on. They will also need to have a stock symbol, which is for identifying the securities. The NYSE uses ticker symbol with either 3 letters or even fewer letters. The American Stock Exchange

(AMEX) and the Nasdaq uses symbol with 4 or more letters and the mutual funds have their symbol ending with an X.

There are also special symbols which appear as additional letters on the symbol, in the case for the NYSE stocks a dot is used for the special securities. Stock symbols that end with Q denote bankruptcy of the issuers. For letter Y, it denotes that the security is an ADR security.

For a full stock symbol, it will show the ticker symbol and the exchange details or the country where it is traded. For instance, if we are trading Microsoft on Nasdaq the details will be as follows; NASDAQ:MSFT. Ticker symbol is derived from the days of old where stock symbol used ticker tape for transmitting prices.

Ticker symbols are essential in facilitating the vast number of trade, which occurs daily around the world. Without stock symbols, investors and brokers are more likely to confuse securities, the issuers and the different securities from the same issuers. Not to forget, ticker symbol through the use of their additional letters or codes; are able to communicate vital information to the investors about the status of the securities being traded.

Meaning of additional letters on a ticker symbol

A- Class A shares, example BRK.A

B- Class B shares, example BRK.B

C- Issuer Qualification Exception, this is when a company does not meet all the listing requirements of exchanges. The company can still remain listed on the exchange for a short period of time.

D- New issue of the existing stock

E- More SEC required filings

F- Foreign issue

G- First convertible bond

H- Second convertible bond

I- Third convertible bond

J- Voting share

K- Non-voting share

L- Miscellaneous for instance foreign preferred, preferred when issued third class warrants and fifth class preferred shares among others

M- Forth class preferred shares

N- Third class preferred shares

O- Second class preferred shares

P- First class preferred shares

Q- In bankruptcy proceedings

R- Rights

S- Shares of beneficial interest

T- With warrants or with rights

U- Units

V- When issued and when distributed; the shares are about to go through a corporate action plan, which has been announced for instance stock split.

W- Warrants

X- Mutual funds

Y- American depository receipt

Z- Miscellaneous situations just like the letter L

OB- Over the counter bulletin board

PK- Pink sheets stock

SC- Nasdaq SmallCap

NM- Nasdaq National Market

As an investor, you ought to carry out thorough investigation on stocks that have the following letters: C, E, L, Q, V and Z. check that the letters are not after the stock symbol before you purchase a particular share in a company.

Types of Stocks You Can Buy

1. Common stock

A majority of stock is distributed as common stock, which shows ownership in a particular company. It also represents a claim on part of the company net profits. Common stockholders have the right to elect a board of directors who are to oversee the management of the corporation.

When compared to most investments, common stock yield a higher return, it also carries a substantial size of risks. This is seen when a company becomes bankrupt, the common shareholders won't receive any money until all the bondholders, preferred shareholders and the creditors are paid. To reduce this risk as an investor; own a variety of well-established stocks, which have a history of good earnings and a solid financial statement; in other words diversify your investments.

2. Preferred stock

Preferred stock shows the degree of ownership an investor has in a company, although it's voting rights is not equivalent to the degree of ownership. The shareholders do not have a voting right; with this share you are guaranteed a fixed dividend. Preferred stock does not offer the same depreciation or appreciation in the price of stocks; therefore, resulting to lower risk and returns.

The benefit with preferred stock is in the event of bankruptcy of the company, the preferred shareholders are paid first before the common shareholders. It is important that you note the creditors and the debt holders will be paid first.

Where to Purchase Stocks

When purchasing stocks, you can get it from an online broker or get assistance from stockbrokers who are licensed to buy securities from you.

Online Brokers

Today online brokers are preferred to the traditional human stockbrokers. The traditional human stockbrokers are also known as investment advisors or registered representatives. Online brokerages cost is based on per share or on per transaction basis, this allows investors to open an account with comparatively low amount of money.

When it comes to online brokers, sign up an account online then transfer funds to the account; it's even simpler than opening a bank account. The moment your account has funds you can start to place your order. You can pick the stocks you want or using the search feature, filter the stocks by criteria. Online brokers include; Charles Schwab Corp., E*Trade, TD Ameritrade and Fidelity Investments. They are the easiest to use and most popular.

Full-Service Brokers

You can also purchase your stocks from a full-service broker, they are traditional stockbrokers. They take time sit with you so as to know you financially and personally. They will look at your lifestyle, risk tolerance, marital status, personality, income, debts and assets and so much more. The full-service brokers will then work hand in hand with you to create a financial plan that best suits your goals, objectives and investments.

Full-service brokers are also able to help you with your tax advice, retirement, budgeting, estate planning and any other financial advice thus the term full-service. These brokers are best for individuals who want everything from one package.

CHAPTER 3: WHAT YOU REQUIRE TO GET STARTED

When it comes to the stock market, it has outperformed investments in Treasury, bill, cash, gold and bonds when it's over a long period of time. In stocks, there are so many ways that you can invest in they include:

- Mutual funds
- Individual stocks
- ETFs
- Domestic or foreign
- Index funds

As an investor you need to understand the different ways of investing. Investing runs from long-term index to short-term trading. It is essential for you to know what kind of an investor are you? Are you a risk taker, risk averse or are you in the middle? Knowing the kind of investor you are will help you to consider the different types of equity investment for instance; index or mutual funds instead of individual stocks.

Index and mutual funds are best for individuals who are uncomfortable in taking risks. This is due to the fact that they are well-diversified and the stocks are different. As a result, it reduces risk and individual stock research.

You need to know the amount of time you can use for investing in order for you to know whether you will invest in stocks, funds or even both. This is dependent on the time that you will be spending in investing. When you carefully select your index or mutual funds, you will then invest your money and leave the hard work of selecting stocks to your fund manager.

When it comes to individual stock, investing in them requires a lot of time. This is because: you are required to make judgments on management, future prospects and earnings. You should be able to differentiate between financial disasters and the money-making stocks, you can do this by knowing their risks, how they make money and their future prospects and so much more.

Diversifying your portfolio

Investors are not to be exposed to only one particular asset. This is seen in the event that you have all your money invested in a small biotech company, then the Food and Drug Administration (FDA) rejects a higher percentage of drugs. Well then your entire portfolio will be impacted negatively.

It is important that you diversify your investment into different sectors, for instance; commodities, consumer goods, insurance and real estates among others. Consider investing across asset classes and keeping some of your money in cash and bonds instead of investing 100% in stocks. You are free to decide on the amount you will invest in, as long as it's in different sectors. As mentioned before, this will lessen the risk of you losing all your money at once.

Stock price is well understood by most people, but it gives inadequate information concerning the value and health of a particular company. For you to get started in the stock market, you need to understand some words that are used. Let's look at them below:

1. **Dividends**

A company can choose to pay dividends when it has reached a certain level of stability and profitability. When a company is still growing, its profits is reinvested so that it continues to grow, but when the growth of the company stabilizes; its dividends can be paid to its shareholders who can still reinvest the dividends in order to acquire more shares of stock.

2. **Outstanding shares**

This is the total number of shares that belong to a company but are held by all of its investors. Outstanding shares are used in calculating other key metrics for instance the Earnings per Share and the Price to Earnings ratio.

3. **Price to Earnings Ratio**

This is also known as price to earnings or P/E, it's the current share price divided by the EPS of the company. With the P/E ratio, you will be able to see what investors are willing pay for their earnings per dollar. It is also a metric that is used to determine if a company is either undervalued or overvalued.

4. **Market capitalization**

This is the current share price which is multiplied by all the outstanding shares. With market capitalization, you are able to have a general idea of the company size. Getting the actual value of a company is more complicated than when you are looking for the market capitalization. You are able to get a better a scale by comparing two market caps than when you are using a share price.

5. **Earnings per share**

This is the total amount of money earned by a company per share of stock. It is obtained by calculating the company's net income minus the dividends on the preferred stock then divided by the average of the outstanding shares.

In other words before you get into the stock market, it's important that you think on what you want to accomplish, how you can do that while still staying within your level of risk tolerance. It also essential that you take note on the amount of time you are able to put in investing. You will also need to choose a broker.

Selecting a Broker

Without a brokerage account, you will not be able to start investing as an investor. When you are deciding on a broker it is not different as to when you are choosing a stock. This is because you will still need a lot of careful scrutiny, plus not all brokers are right for each and every investor.

When it comes to brokers, there are two types of brokers; regular brokers and broker-resellers. Regular brokers deal directly with their client while broker-resellers act as an intermediary; that is between the larger broker and the client. Regular brokers are known to be more reliable than the broker-resellers, although this does not mean that all broker-resellers are naturally bad, no instead you need to investigate them before signing up with them.

There are regular brokers who are members of the, Securities Investor Protection Corporation and the Financial Industry Regulatory Authority (FINRA). Such brokers include; TD Ameritrade, Fidelity and Capital One Investing.

Factors to Consider When Selecting A Broker

1. Full-service or discount/online brokers

Full-service brokers offer more services to the investors; they are the ones doing a lot of legwork. Investors are able to obtain one-on-one advice, personal suggestions and research from the brokers. Discount brokers give you an option of asking a broker for advice on a particular trade using your brokerage account. The limitation in this is that you will need to pay some amount of money as the execution fees.

2. Cost and fees

Beside the trade execution fees, there are also other brokerage fees that you ought to consider. They include:

- ➤ Minimums- most of the brokers have a minimum amount of money that they require from you, in order for you to have a brokerage account. The amount ranges from $ 500 to $1000 for the online discount brokers.

- ➤ Margin- most investors opt out of opening a margin account straight away, although in future it's something to put into consideration. The margin accounts require a high minimum balance when compared to the standard brokerage accounts. Ensure that you check the interest charged when you make a trade on margin.

➤ Withdrawal- although it's your money, there are times when it is hard for you to make a withdrawal. This happens when brokers have fees on withdrawing or they won't allow withdrawing if your balance will be below the minimum amount required. Therefore, it is essential that you understand the rules in withdrawing money from an account with your potential broker.

Most brokers have a similar fee structure; there are some with a complex fee structure which makes it hard to sort out the hidden fees. This is more common in broker-resellers who use the fee structure to entice their clients. In the event that you have a broker with an unusual fee structure, ascertain if the broker is legitimate. The fee structure should be able to meet up with your investing style and look out for your interests.

The kind of broker you select is determined by the kind of investor that you are. Therefore, it is wise for you to first determine your investment style before investing.

Opening an Account

For you to start trading you need to open a trading account with your broker. It's the trading account that allows investment in the stock market, with the account you can buy or sell stocks. The following is how you can open an account:

- Select a stock firm of broker, the broker ought to be good and takes your order timely as time is very important in stock market.
- Compare the rates of brokerage, as every broker charges a certain amount of fee that is for processing your orders.
- Some brokers offer discount depending on the trade conducted, before opening an account considers this. You do not have to choose a broker with the lowest fees as good brokerage services can tend to have higher charges than normal.
- Get in touch with a brokerage firm so as to enquire about your account opening process.

Usually a firm sends its representative with an account opening and a Know Your Client (KYC) form.

- Fill the two forms and attach them with two documents which serve as evidence of your address and identity.

- Verification of your information will be done either through the phone, you will be asked to give your personal details or through an in-person check.

- When your documents are processed, you will be given your trading account details. You will then be able to trade in the stock market.

Documents in Opening an Account

When opening an account there are documents that you will need to submit, a proof of identity and your address, a passport size picture and an account opening form that is for opening your trading account. For a proof of identity you can use; voter's ID, telephone bill and an IT returns; proof of address you can use; Ration card, voter ID card or a driving license among others.

Some of The Online Brokers You Can Use

As an investor it is essential that you have the best online brokers that you can trade with. Online stock broker can be known by their inexpensive stock trades, their powerful trading tools or by their award-winning customer service. The following is a list of online brokers you can use to invest in:

1. TD Ameritrade

The TD Ameritrade was rated as the number 1 Broker for traders' 2018 by the stockBrokers.com; its stock trade is $6.95. It is the first broker to be able to support 24 hours and five days in a week of trade. Its platform that is the thinkorswim was the number 1 desktop platform, its tool, research, customer service, education, mobile apps are all the award winning. Its current offer is a free trade for 60 days and be able to get up to $600

2. Fidelity

This brokerage firm is known for its value driven customer experience, its regular stock is simply $4.95each. Fidelity broker was number 1 in ratings due to their order execution quality, which is able to drive down the trading costs even lower. Fidelity also was number 1 in research tool; it's the only broker which offers 12 third-party research reports for specific equities. It has viewpoint articles that are at the top of the class.

3. **TradeStation**

TradeStation presents the most advanced desktop trading platform there is in the industry. Investors with a previous experience in the market will feel at home due to its competitive commission rates; that are on the stocks and the options trading. It has the best platform technology

4. **E*TRADE**

This is the best broker for option trading due to its OptionHouse platform which also has mobile apps. Their OptionHouse was rated the number 1platform for the trade of options for seven years. It also has a number 1 rating for their Mobile Trading in StockBrokers.com 2018 review.

They charge the same way the TD Ameritrade charges that is $6.95 for each trade, although they offer a discount of $4.95 when you place in the least 30 trades per quarter.

The 4 brokers in the list above are just some of the brokerage firms that you can use. As an investor it is very important for you to have the best stock broker in order for your needs to be met.

CHAPTER 4: HOW TO FIND GOOD STOCKS AND HOW TO BUY AND SELL STOCKS

What is the price?

Just like the commodity markets, the stocks are priced into the value of a firm. Think of how the Apple Company prices their MacBook computers or the iPhones. Each product is priced according to the quality and the consumer preferences. For a company such as Apple, whose brand recognition and reputation is undoubtful, it is more likely to attract big sales from its targeted consumer group. Apple company has specifically set premium prices for its products which are manufactured with state of the art security features and are generally perceived to be superior brand to other technology giants such as SamSung. The perception of higher quality and brand recognition has landed Apple a leverage in the manufacture of electronic products and provision of technological services such as the iTunes and cloud computing. Using Apple.Inc as an example, we can now delve into the depths of understanding what the price of a stock is and what determines it.

The price, in the context of the stock market, is the lowest financial commitment a buyer is willing to make to acquire the stock of a firm. It is also the highest price that a stock holder can sell his or her stake to gain a financial value from the stock market as defined by (Kramer, 2018). The narrated case example of the Apple Company is a good example to explain how the stock prices are determined. The prices of the stocks for the different companies are determined in a stock exchange market such as the New York Exchange, Nasdaq, to mention a few. The stock listings of the companies have a prerequisite criterion, which underlines the requirements that a company must meet in order to feature in a certain stock market. After the Initial Public Offer (IPO), the firms attract stock buyers from various investors depending on its market valuations and the brand image. Corporate leadership, for instance, is a good metric that is used to value the stocks of a company. Investors are more willing to engage in trading the stocks of a company that has a good reputation in its managerial level and product offering in the market. The market capitalization measures the company worth depending on the stock price and the outstanding shares held by all the shareholders.

How are the stock prices and market capitalization determined?

For the company stocks, the determination of the price value of the stocks begins with the IPO. A firm, for example, Facebook, approaches an investment bank and pays for the process of valuation of its stocks through the complex calculations conducted by the financial institution. Valuation helps in deriving the worth of the company, the so-called market capitalization. The stock prices are then determined from this capitalization. The "market cap" is derived by obtaining the product of the stock price and the outstanding shares of the company. The outstanding shares is the share capital that is held by the shareholders, inclusive of the share blocks that are held by the institutional investors and those that belong to the company insiders as well as the officials.

For the determination of the stock price, let us assume that Microsoft Corporation, listed as MSFT has a trading value of $60.57, given that the outstanding shares of the company are valued at $6.7 billion, the total market value of the company will be $ 405.819 billion. The stock prices are instrumental in determining the market capitalization of a company. This means that a drop in the stock price would also see the market value of the company drop significantly. This is the reason why the investors are interested in the stock prices for their outstanding shares because they determine whether they gain or lose in their stock investments. The price movements marked by the increase or decrease in the stock prices are determined by the economic factors such as the demand and supply that accrue to the company shares traded in the stock market. The market sentiments about the performance of a company are also instrumental in determining the pricing of the stocks for the publicly listed companies.

Purchasing a stock

Purchasing a stock is a decision that has to be made by the market participants in the stock market depending on the preferable market conditions. Of course, before buying any stock, the market information has to support the buying behavior. The stock market goes through a series of buying and selling with effect from the market sentiments, the market capitalization of the listed companies and the profit motive of generating wealth to the shareholders. The decision criteria that we have to look at here is therefore, when do you purchase a stock? It is not a straightforward answer question. There is more than just finding the right answer for this question preferably because there are many considerations investors have to make before they can eventually buy a stock.

The investors may choose to buy a stock that is on the selloff. In this case, the investors want to make sure that they buy at relatively lower prices, with a future anticipation of the value gain in the stocks of a company. The level of the prices for a company's stock are analyzed with the regard to the future expectations. If the investors have to consider buying the stocks when they have a low value, they must have the anticipation that the company will make good financial progress in the future and the stocks will rise in price. Therefore, the price alone is not a good criterion that is used for the buying of stocks. Other economic indicators pointing out to the probability of future growth are more fundamental. Factors such as the low debt ratio, prevailing economic conditions, undervalued stock, are all possible indicators of a buying decision.

The price movements are presented in form of charts in the stock markets. It is upon the investors to do their analysis on the market charts to determine at what prices they should trigger a buy position. The stock traders should have a target that is well marked out in the financial markets. A good stock will indicate chart patterns that are indicative of a buying trend. It is upon the investors to target their buying positions upon which the market is anticipated to favor the buys. The chart patterns are one of the fundamentally important technical tools that are used by the investors to determine where the stock prices are most likely to move next. By analyzing the charts, the investors are able to come up with price targets they will buy into in a bullish trending market. Many of the stock traders would agree to the common phrase that "the trend is your friend". The trend of the market charts tells a lot about the value and the pricing of the companies' stocks. When the markets are trencing hard with a positive bullish momentum, the investors should enter buy positions because it is indicative of a good stock that has a preferably healthy financial trending.

When analyzing the market trends, it is important that the stock traders evaluate corrective pullbacks within an uptrend market. An uptrend market is a stock market that shows that the stock prices of a company are moving up. This happens when there is increase in the economic and financial performance of a company. Factors such as increase in net profits, expansion of portfolio and good prospects of a company's growth contribute to this trend, which shows higher highs and lower highs price movements and chart patterns formation (Luo et al., 2015). The investors are therefore supposed to be careful of the chart patterns that indicates declining trend for the market stocks to avoid buying into a losing stock. Another indicator of the purchasing decision for a stock is undervaluation.

When a stock is undervalued, the projected future cash flows are slightly higher than the current market prices. This means that a company's stock will be higher priced in the future as expressed in the discounted terms as compared to the present price tag. Such an analysis is good for the investors because they are able to anticipate the price movements and make their trading decisions. The investors tend to avoid stocks whose prices are very low because it evidences a company that is poorly performing or on the verge of collapsing. Sometimes, buying higher is necessary out of the expectation that a company whose stock prices are going up is a reflection of good financial health.

Selling a Stock

It has been earlier mentioned that the stock market moves through a series of buying and selling. Historical comparison of chart data is indicative of the same patterns of buying and selling. It is important to mark out selling as one of the undertakings that have great influence in the financial markets and determine what influence does the selling pressures have in the stock markets. Just like buying, caution should be taken not to sell into a stock that would soon gain value and force you into losses. Investors have to make their decisions wisely and should not time the stock markets. It is not wise to wait until the market charts reach their top most part to sell a stock neither is it credible to buy when the prices for a stock are at the absolute bottom.

It is good to sell a stock when the initial investment decision is no longer viable. In this case, the stock is sold when a stock trader realizes that the market no longer favors the direction he had anticipated. Should a trader feel that there is something wrong with the fundamental decision he had made while purchasing a stock, then it is good to sell into the buy position to avoid possible losses. This decision is important because traders are likely to experience losses when there is a sharp turn in the market direction. Sometimes the stock market moves out of a hype especially from the media about the stock valuations of a company (Little, 2018). Such a hype would cause the novice traders to buy positions of the existing stock prices spontaneously pushing the prices higher. However, the long-term trend for the stocks is not sustained and only plummets after some time when the news impact has faded out. Such occurrences should be well evaluated and if a trader buys stocks in that nature of the market he should consider selling them.

The selling in the stock market should also be established by evaluating the relation between the price and the valuation. If the current price is far higher than the P/E ratio for a considerable period of time, say five years, the investor should consider selling the stocks (Wong, Chew & Sikorski, 2015). Prices higher than the typical P/E over the considered period indicates that the stocks may be selling in the near future if they cannot sustain their growth. Facebook and Apple are some of the companies that have been growing rapidly. It is good time that the investors started selling those shares and looking into other companies that have the potential of growth in the future. A sustained increase in the stock prices over a significant period is indicative that a company is performing well but the stocks may suddenly be subject to market shocks should an unfavorable outcome happen for the best performing company. The shareholders pull out in large numbers and the stock buyers are forced into losses. It is therefore, wise for the stock buyers to sell some of their stocks when a company is doing well in the market to book some profits before the market turns against them.

Sometimes the reasons for selling the stocks may not be limited to the market forces. There are times when a stock shareholder may feel the need to liquidate some of his/her stock holdings for personal needs. Financially, an individual has many needs at any given time. Maybe, you would like to settle some college fees or pending medical bills and the only probable source of income is the stocks held. Selling these stocks will provide the money needed to meet the individual wants. It would also be wise to sell the stocks when a stock shareholder realizes that the company he holds stocks has embarked on a plan to reduce its operational costs. Laying off the workforce is one of the fundamental indicators of a firm that is working down on its costs. Such undertakings are indicative of a firm that may be experiencing financial struggles although the stock prices are likely to be going higher in the short term.

CHAPTER 5: PROTECTING YOUR STOCKS INVESTMENT

What Is A Stock Investment?

A stock is a form of security that shows that the holder claims part of a firm's assets as well as earnings. A shareholder may choose whether to invest in the common shares or the preferred ones. For the common shares, a shareholder has more rights as compared to the preferred shares. The shareholder is entitled to voting rights and also receives dividends as they accrue. The preferred stocks owners have no rights to vote in the company's general meetings but have a higher claim on the company's assets and incomes than the common shareholders. Their dividends are paid earlier and when a company liquidates they receive the payment for their shares first. The shareholder's collection of stocks is his/her stock investment portfolio. Portfolio investment is passive in nature and involves the investors buying sizeable securities of a company for a later claim on the dividends as the company generates income. This investment is undertaken with the expectation that a company will make profits in the future and the value of the stock will gain value so that the shareholder redeems them at a higher value to make profits.

The portfolio investments are not limited to stocks. Investors can also invest in Treasury bills, bonds issued by the government, real estate, or buy corporate bonds. The investment decisions are made based on a number of viable factors. For instance, a stock holder may need to establish his tolerance level for the risk involved in investing in stocks. The level of the amount an investor is willing to invest in the stock market also determines the kind of stocks to be bought. For monied investors, good stocks with viable prospects of growth should be adopted. If an investor does not have the financial muscle to single out stocks, he/she should try a conservative investment especially with the mutual funds that buy stocks on behalf of the investors and generates wealth to the shareholders. For the institutional investors, the stocks should have a long-term growth trajectory so that they are able to generate more income and offset their liabilities. Due to the risky nature of the stock investments, the idea of protecting these investments therefore becomes a critical undertaking for financial success of shareholders and other investors.

Why Do The Investors Need To Protect Their Stock Investment?

The idea of protection should probably be the first thing that stock shareholders think of even before venturing into the stock market. The market is sometimes vulnerable to the market shocks that will cause the stocks to suddenly lose value. It is therefore important that the stock holders come up with appropriate methods to cushion them against the unexpected turns in the market. The idea of stock protection is not new. Walmart have a remarkable instance in history where its stocks lost terribly and the world continues to learn a lesson on the nature of the stock markets to the current day. The stock markets' gravitational forces are disastrous and can drive the prices in the opposite direction in a short time generating huge losses to the stock holders. It is always prudent that whenever an investor has some bids on stock holdings to protect them against the unimaginable consequences of the stock markets. Dow fell by 23% in 1987, a rare event in the stock markets history (Harris, 2017). This shows that any outcome is a probable event and that every decision to be made in investing in the stocks should be well thought out.

Stocks are open to the exogenous events that can sharply lead to the fall in their value. Gaining stocks are also subject to the market fright whereby the investors are afraid that the stocks will pull down since the Wall Street fateful day. For instance, the Morningstar Director, Christine Benz, was quoted in Forbes magazine saying that, "Many people have become complacent because this bull market has gone on for so long", (Diane Harris, 2017). The investment in stocks should also be protected based on the duration that individual wishes to hold. For instance, retired investors would buy short term assets, with less risk as opposed to long term assets that might be bought by the young people who have the time to make up for the losses incurred. The investment time horizon is therefore another consideration to put in place to ensure that the trading decisions are secure. When investing on long term basis, the investors should make sure they have the stocks that have the probability of generating value and preferably immune to the short-term market shocks.

Short term stocks attract more risk and is important for the stock investors to choose the stock assets well to avoid market volatility risks that may cause huge losses. Protecting an investment in the stocks becomes a critical factor because it determines the value of the investment in the long term and also cushions against the exogenous shocks which are difficult to predict.

Methods Used In Protecting The Stock Investment

Rebalancing Portfolio

It is good for an investor to have stocks investment that alternate in their earnings so that even when some of the stock do not gain value and others do, the stock holder will still experience growth in his portfolio. The diversification of the stock assets is not a new concept and it is used to justify the spread of risks so that no single stock carries a significant huge risk that could lead to unanticipated losses. Diversification helps in spreading the risk of losing to more than one assert so that for the stock assets that are likely to lose, there are others that will offset the loss by gaining value and possibly lead to overall growth for the stock portfolio held by the stockholder. For instance, the technology stocks have been gaining in S&P 500 for the better part of the year by 25.4 % proportion. As a stock trader, it is the right time to pull off some profits from these stock markets and look for other low yielding stocks that have a better chance of growth in the future. The S&P 500 has a weighted average of around 23.5% in stocks. If a trader has a stock value that is higher than the average market value, then it is the time he sells part of the stock to reclaim some profits and reduce the risk of being tipped off in market drawdowns.

Buying stocks that have low volatility

There are stocks that have low volatility even in unstable markets. The stocks that have stability such as the McDonald's that has been trading at an average price value of (MCD, $159.10). The stocks for the company are traded by USMV, which is a fund company. The company has been stable despite the market volatility. It has maintained an average of 2.3 points annual proportion in percentages.

Investing in stocks that are not correlated

Stocks are subject to systemic risks that should be avoided in making investment decisions. This starts from dealing with different kinds of the stocks such as the commodities, bonds, currencies, or the real estate.

The mix of the investment portfolio ensures that the trader is immune from the market uncertainties that are associated with a particular type of the stock. This kind of approach is important in minimizing the so called systemic risks. The systemic risks expose a stock trader to losses if one of the stock assets has a significant relationship to the other stock held. When an unfavorable market condition causes one of the stocks to lose value, all the other stocks are also similarly affected. If the portfolio of the trader is not diversified into varied stock assets, huge losses will be suffered. A turn out of the market unprecedented events or sentiments against a certain stock may cause huge losses as it occurred in Black Monday for the Wall Street in the history of stock trading.

Use of Leap Puts or other alternatives

Put options are useful for the future likelihood that the prices will decline. These kind of stocks acts as a cushion to the fall in prices for the stocks that a stock trader holds in the future. The put options are set for selling at a predetermined price level in the future such that when the stocks decline in value, the stock holder can compensate any chance of a loss. For instance, if the stock prices have risen to unexpected levels such as from $80 to $102 within a short period, then the stock trader can buy the put option at around $105 for a specified period of expiry, say 6 months. Before the option reaches expiry at the specified time, the trader can sell off to offset a probable decline in the stock prices to avoid incurring losses. The put options may not necessarily lead to the realization of profits but cushion the losses in case of unexpected turns in unfavorable direction in the stock markets. Other options such as the LEAPS are also useful to offset the likelihood of losing in the stock markets. These instruments are bought on a considerable long-term basis. The securities provide protection against the losses in loss of value for the stocks for as long as 3 years. Investors considering buying stocks on a long-term period can therefore considering securing such an instrument.

Use of a Stop Loss

Stock traders can avoid incurring heavy losses in the stock markets by placing hard stops. This is a predetermined price that a sell order is triggered for the declining stocks. This price is not altered under any market condition, it is fixed. Let us assume that a stock has been bought at $12, and the stock trader has set his stop loss at $10. If the price for the bought stock declines below the purchasing price and hits the $10, the sell order is triggered automatically and further losses stopped. This kind of an approach to the stock market is conservative and is often used by the stock traders who feel that the stock market is a big risk and they need to protect their stock portfolio before they are plunged into unimaginable limits. The trailing stops are another option similar to the hard stops. For the trailing stop, it moves higher as the prices increase. If it is set at $10 and the price moves at $12, the trailing stop will move higher, say to $10.50. This cushions the stock trader against losses and books in some small profits should the prices drop lower, say, to $9. However, if this happens to be a pull back and the prices again moves higher, it is disadvantageous in that the market gains are forfeited.

Investing in dividend paying stocks

If a shareholder buys stocks from a company that pays significant portion of their returns as dividends to the investors, he/she will be cushioned against the losses in the market. A dividend acts as a security to the bought stock because the gains gained through dividends offset the market losses though sometimes partly. The other side of the coin is that when companies pay good dividends, the investors are more willing to buy their stocks. This gives them an advantage of growing their capital and stock quickly. Therefore, for the dividend yielding stocks, the stock holder has some level of protection and can rarely lose significantly from the stock markets.

CHAPTER 6: HOW MUCH MONEY YOU NEED TO START INVESTING IN STOCKS

When investing in stocks, you need enough money to be able to open a brokerage account. Be able to buy a share of stock no to forget paying your commission fee. When it comes to online brokers for instance; E*TRADE you require a minimum of $500 so as to open a brokerage account with them.

For TD Ameritrade you do not require a minimum amount of cash for you to open an account. As a result, when it comes to TD Ameritrade, you can only require $10 then with $3 you can be able to invest in one particular share of stock. TD Ameritrade charges $6.95 as their commission fee.

For you to be successful in investing you need to have $10 to $20 in the least. This is because, if you only have enough for buying a one or two shares, then paying your commission from your earnings will sternly eat into them. Buying stocks in small quantities makes your commission fee eat into a lot of your gains, thus making it hard for you to actually make profit.

Saving up so as to have large quantities of share for instance, 10 shares in the least will work to your advantage. This will be seen as your commission will cost lesser per cost of share, with the 10 shares your commission will be $1.39 this includes the buying and selling commission. With 10 shares you will need stocks to increase to up to 14% in order for you to attain break-even; instead of the 68% that you will have in purchasing 2 shares. Break-even price decreases with the increase in the number of shares that you purchase.

The Minimum in Opening an Account

When you are opening an account, you may think that all you need is to visit a brokerage firm and then open an account. What most people are not aware of is that all the financial institutions have a minimum deposit that investors need to pay. This means that you will not be able to open an account until you make some deposit; this goes to the point where with a small amount of $100, you will not open an account in some brokerage firms. Let's look at some of things that you can invest in:

Stocks

As seen earlier, there are two types of stockbrokers that is, the discount and full-service brokers. When it comes to the full-service brokers, you can have $25,000 and above as the minimum account size. Therefore, investors with $1000 will be left with the discount brokers as there option. The discount brokers have a lower fee, although you do not expect a lot from them that is in the sense of hand holding as seen in full-service brokers.

Discount brokers have a lower fee because as an investor you are responsible for your investment decisions. You cannot ask for investment advice from the discount brokers, with the $1000 you will have some of the discount brokers taking you while others will not. Therefore, you will need to shop around.

With the Direct Stock Purchase Plans (DSPPs), you can be able to buy shares directly from a cooperative. You may have some of companies with a minimum initial investment, which has amount restrictions of $100 to

$500. With the start of online trading, there are a good number of discount brokers who have no minimum deposit. However, you will have restrictions and a higher fee on certain types of trades, it's important for an investor to consider this when investing in stocks.

The Cost of Investing
Commissions

It is vital for you to consider the expense that you will experience in purchasing your investments, the moment your account will be open. When you are buying an investment, you will incur some cost known as commissions. If your funds are limited, then transaction fee can put a hole in your $1000.

With a constant trade, investing in stocks can be quite costly, especially when you have a small amount of money to invest. Whenever you trade stock, either by buying or selling it, there is a trading fee that you will incur. When it comes to trading fees you will have $5 per trade as the lowest amount and $10 per trade on the high end.

Trade is an order of purchasing shares in a company; therefore, if you are purchasing 5 different stocks although at the same time. It will still be taken as 5 different trades, thus you will be charged for each of the five trades. In the event that you purchase stocks from 5 different companies with $1000, you will have a trading cost of $50 this is equal to 5% of the $1000.

In case you fully invest the $1000, your money will be reduced to $950 after your trading cost being removed. This also represents a loss of 5% yet you have not even had a chance of earning a single cent; selling of these stocks will again cost you some amount of money that is another $50. This means, buying and selling of the 5 stocks will roughly cost you $100 or 10% of your $1000 deposit. In case your investment does not earn enough to cover for the trading cost, you will end up losing money by simply entering and existing the trade.

It is possible to invest in stocks with just a small amount of money. Investing in stocks is more complicated than the selection of the right investments (which is also a difficult task), you ought to be aware of the limitations that as an investor you will face. It is very important for you to do your homework, know the minimum amount required by the brokers and compare the commission with the other brokers. With a small amount of money you will not be able to purchase cost effective stocks and still diversify your portfolio.

When investing, invest the amount of money you are willing to lose and be able to live like you never had the money anyway. You can start with $1000, so that in the event that you lose it, your lifestyle will not be affected. The minimum amount that you can invest in largely depends on your broker's fee, although $1000 is usually recommended, you can still do $500 if you are planning on adding more to the account.

Golden Rules of Investing In Stock Markets

When it comes to stock market, it can be an easy or a challenging investment. Stock market can be a big hit if you are aware of the games' rules. Investors here are able to learn from their mistakes and graduate to becoming smart investors.

The stock market always rewards investors who learn from their mistakes. As an investor in stock market you require discipline and patience. A lot of investors make a loss as they lack patience and discipline, which are critical factors when it comes to stock trading. Beside patience and discipline there are golden rules that investor need to follow for their success in stock market they include:

1. **Investing in a business you understand**

As an investor, never invest in a stock but rather invests in the business itself. It is vital for an investor to invest in a business that he understands. Before investing in corporations ensure that you understand the business that the company is into.

2. **Buying low and selling high**

The response of the market and the unexpected news leads to selling of stocks which never gets swayed. As a matter of fact, when everybody is selling their stock you should on the other hand be buying. This is the time when you need to have cash with you, when there is a fall it ought to be a purchasing opportunity for you. This is not an easy thing to do, although the moment you attain it you will be able to make a lot of the market.

Buying low allows you have a low cost of holding and be able to have a bigger percentage in the event that the market increases. It is then that you can be able to make

A majority of investors lc
ability to be able to con
greed and fear. When it c
enticement of making quic
resist. Their greed increas
of great returns made in
period of time. This will e
being speculative, resultin
unknown companies wit
that are present.

Instead of the investors n
their fingers when there is
market. The bear market
investors panic, selling
prices. Hence, when it c
fear are the worst emotion
if you are not guided by th

4. Creating a broad portfolio

When it comes to earning optimum returns on your investments at a much lower risk, diversification of your portfolio through the asset classes and instruments is the main factor to consider. The level of risk diversification is dependent on the capacity of the investor to take risks.

5. Investing with your surplus funds

If you are going to take risks in an unpredictable market such as stock, then it is important that you ensure that you first have surplus funds that you can afford to lose. It isn't compulsory for you to lose your money in the current scenario; your investments are able to give you gains within months. When it comes to the stock market, no one can be 100% sure that is why as investors you need to take risks.

6. Having a realistic approach

It is not wrong for you as an investor to hope for the best when it comes to your investments. Although having hope is different from having unrealistic assumptions. As an example, a lot of stocks have generated 50% returns in the great Bull Run over the recent years. This however does not imply that you will always have 50% returns from the stock market.

7. Following a disciplined investment approach

In the history of stock market, even the great bull runs have shown sessions of panic moments. The instability seen in the market has unavoidably made investors lose their money in spite of the great bull runs. Nevertheless, investors who place their money in the market systematically in appropriate shares, then patiently held on to the investment have outstanding returns generated. Consequently the importance of having patience and following a disciplined investment method, that is apart from having a long-term picture.

8. Do not try to time the market

Timing the market is a no for the investors. The investors instead can try to know the price level that is appropriate to individual shares. Financial planners always discourage investors from timing the market. This is because it's a sure way for them to lose their hard-earned money.

Therefore do not try to time the market, as to date no one has been able to successfully and consistently be able to time the stock market cycle correctly. A myth that is common in the stock market and will remain so in the future is catching of the tops and bottoms. With this myth, a lot of people have lost their money compared to the number of individuals who have earned money.

9. Make informed decisions

Always ensure that you do a proper research before you start to invest in stocks. Investors rarely do this, as they go with the name of the company or with the industry to which they belong in. using this kind of approach is a wrong way of putting your money in the stock market.

10. Avoid herd mentality

When it comes to a typical buyer, their decisions are usually influenced by his neighbors, relatives or acquaintances. This is seen when a majority of individual are investing in a certain stock, an investor may have a tendency of investing in the same stock.

This kind of strategy will eventually go wrong in the long run.

CONCLUSION

When it comes to investing in stocks, we have seen that you can start investing with as little as $1000. You also need to have in mind the rate of commission that a broker would be charging. For you to basically start in investing in stocks, it is mandatory for you to have a brokerage account. It is where you can choose whether to be represented by a broker or not. If you are represented by a broker, is he a full-service or a discount broker.

As an investor before you actually start to invest in the stock market, it is vital for you to understand how the stock market works. You can do this by actually knowing the kind of business the company you are going to buy shares deal with. When it comes to stock market, this is one the surest ways that you can invest your money for a long term investment such as retirement.

The stock market has outperformed investments such as; bonds, treasury bills, gold and cash. Investing in stocks can either be long-term or short-term. Long-term investment gives investors a higher chance of earning revenue compared to short-term, which an investor have high chances of making a loss.

When you know the kind of investor that you are in the stock market is very important. Are you a risk taker, in the middle or risk averse; this will help you in determining the type of equity that you can invest in. know the amount of time that you can allocate for your investment, the amount of time that you have will tell if you can invest in funds, stocks or even both of them.

As an investor you need to know stock investment is unstable, thus the reason why long-term investment being more appropriate. Ensure that you have your emotions of fear and greed in check as they are a big cause of you losing your investments. It is very important, as an investor that you are able differentiate a financial disaster and a money-making stock. You can be able to do this by being able to determine the risks, how they earn money and the future prospects that a company has.

Not to forget the golden rules that you need to adhere to for you to be successful in the stock market. The rules include; not investing with your emotions, not timing the market, following a disciplined investment approach, having a realistic approach and investing in a business that you understand among others. Following the golden rules is important in ensuring that your investment in the stock market is a success.